# TEN

*The New Indian Poets*

NIRALA SERIES

# TEN

## *The New Indian Poets*

*Selected & Edited by*

**JAYANTA MAHAPATRA**

**& YUYUTSU SHARMA**

NIRALA

Nirala Publications
G.P.O. Box 7004
Daryaganj, New Delhi-110002
niralabooks@yahoo.co.in
www.niralapublications.com

First Edition 2013

ISBN-81-8250-025-7



**Cover Design : S.A.A. Wasti**

Cover Photo, *The Mask*,
By New York-based Regina Walker, currently hanging
in the Staten Island Museum in New York



Printed at
H.S. Offset Printers
New Delhi-110002

# Contents

# TEN

*The New Indian Poets*

# ONE

# Anupama Raju

Published widely, **Anupama Raju** is a writer and translator. Her poems feature in the forthcoming *Harper Collins' Anthology of Modern Indian Poetry* (2011). She is the writer for a collaborative Indo-French Poetry and Photography Project (2012). Anupama's first book of poems, *Nine* is forthcoming from Daastaan. Anupama currently lives in Trivandrum, India, where she works as a corporate trainer and freelance journalist.

## Wake up

Shall I wake you with tears
of my dead poem? Frozen word
seeking warmth in deceptive fears

caught in forgotten lines, it appears,
cold memory fleeting like a sunbird.
Shall I wake you with tears

falling from lonely eyes of wild deer
roaming forests – unknown, unfurled?
Close, yet far from deceptive fears

breathing a dying wind that smears
red over weary paths of my shepherd.
Come, I shall wake you with tears

of my dead poem where lived seers
with spirits born of reasons absurd
and lead you to my mind, still for years

till you come, touch, hold these tears
alive to songs of pain rightfully churned
by sleeping eyes. I shall wake you with tears
of my dead poem to live again, far from fears.

## No borders

**1.**

Poems sit on walls.
Moss-covered words fall gently
on my neighbor's page.

**2.**

That yellow page has wings.
Van Gogh blue plumes fly across
seas named in old books.

**3.**

I travel with those
books inside, metal boxes
dancing on shy waves.

**4.**

Waves lick distant shores,
land of a virgin language
looking for my tongue.

**5.**

My tongue speaks mango
words, yellow with ripe meanings.
Drip into islands.

**6.**

Islands float, brushing
against each other without
passports. No limits.

**7.**

No limits here. Where
suns dip into syllables,
orange clouds hitch-hike.

**8.**

Clouds, budget travelers
seeking summer tan under
sun-dried similes.

**9.**

Similes wave from
a passing ship that sails to
those empty countries.

**10.**

Empty countries wait.
Bowls that long for fish swimming
across language lakes.

**11.**

I become a lake
but no lotus blooms in here
only poems of yore.

**12.**

My poems sit on walls
watch over neighbors, countries.
Poems have no borders.

## House of dreams

I've heard it all before. A story shaped by:
wealth, fame and tradition,
Brick, tiles and wood,
That went into ruin years before I was born.

About the great Ambady tharawad.
"Oh, we're from the great Ambady" *Ammoomma* said.
Ambady whose ghosts still hover around Trichur's Elite Hotel.
Ambady where prosperity once danced
Where they grew up on *velyammoomma's chammanthi choru*.
Where happiness laughed at the doorstep
When suddenly massive teak doors closed
and opened to decades of bad fortune.

It's a family curse that ate into Ambady.
A parasite that fed on those prosperous times,
till the grand old matriarch crumbled under.
And history settled in, like fungus.

But the great Ambady still survives
- in disillusioned, withering minds who still
know that musty feel, that woody smell of history.

- And in me, as I dream in delirious delight
Of Ambady whose ghosts still hover around Trichur's Elite Hotel.
Ambady where prosperity once danced.

*Tharawad: Ancestral home*

*Chammanthi choru: Rice mixed with coconut chutney*

## When a god dances with me

There stands my brown-eyed one
sweeping me in his divine gaze
beautiful arms holding up the earth
where I bloom wet in a dreamy monsoon
filling snowy mountains, home to wild rivers
where I first saw him swimming naked
my untamed god of virility.

Hear me, my curly-haired one,
come and play me, your solitary flute
and drink from the music of desire
deep dense dark like the night
free from blinding morals of day.
Come, my Shiva, come my Krishna
let us dance our way into a new world.

Let us destroy what we created.

# Tale of a forest

## I

Love drinks me dry, yet I smell like rain
pungent wet earth almost washed away
by a passing storm that drifted lifeless
but lived in me long enough to die
quietly one day, leaving a seed here
a leaf there, a thinning forest.

## II

No flowers bloom in this forest
No. Yet I smell like ranting rain.
Lonely trees make their home in here
singing of a season not far away.
But do not trust spring, it too will die
quietly one day like words: lifeless.

## III

Meanings lie cold like cobbles, lifeless
And lost in streams, once rivers in this forest.
Warriors of pain, they fight still, not willing to die.
Courage warms me, so I smell like the rain
pouring from eyes dreaming of loves far away
now dancing under a moon, afraid to rise here.

## IV

Night swallowed the moon, spilling black here
but stars will always shine, smile. Never lifeless
is this kingdom, born to keep evil eyes away
but close to protect secrets of the forest
where I will always smell like the rain
where dreams shall breed, unwilling to die.

## V

When dreams breed, desires don't die
but softly feed on the grass growing here,

grass that sprouts when I smell like the rain
and flow down hills, remembering a storm, lifeless
now breathing through hidden pathways of the forest
that shall never lead you home, too far away.

**VI**

Home was almost always far away
for many a traveller who came to die
in the lure of the fruit of my forest
that still hangs unplucked, untried here.
Fear not my gentle offerings, leave them not lifeless.
But taste me now, for I smell like the rain.

Thus speaks a voice not years away
from a rain that will die
when the storm leaves here, this aching forest.

## Born, again

Yesterday, I died:
In the teacup you broke,
spilling years of love.
In the letter you wrote
of a love once alive.

Yesterday I died:
In the green, green grass.
In the footsteps that measured
three and a thousand years.

Yesterday I died:
In the sliced onion
rotting in a dark kitchen.
In the lazy pile of dust
Swept by wrinkly fingers.

Yesterday I died.

And today, in my place stands
A papery young rose
With dew on its petals
And the sun by its thorns.

## No 1, Bombay Flats

Lazy old doors wake up to a rusty doorbell
ringing, roaring, raving as I enter
a world lit by a sleepy bulb and a yellow wall.
Smell of fried fish, coconut oil, old books
sleeps in the apartment, lulled by humming cobwebs.
Dust and dirt live in happy harmony.
All twirling in circles of a dead silence
till a precious voice called out from a rocking chair,
where sat Appoopan, shining in his white mundu
soaring, sparkling, spilling into my eyes
Till I could no longer see him.

What remains is the last drop of his dead smile.

TWO

# Rabindra K Swain

Poet and translator, **Rabindra K Swain** (1960) has published four books of poems including *Susurrus in the Skull*. His critical works include *Silent Tongues: Writings in Contemporary Indian Poetry*. His poems have been published in *Times Literary Supplement, Critical Quarterly, World Literature Today, The Kenyon Review, The Literary Review, Verse; Ariel, Chandrabhaga, The Little Magazine*, etc. He lives in Bhubaneswar.

# Susurrus in the Skull

This is then the skull,
I mean the one inside my head,
I thought, looking at a drawing
of a skeleton in the dictionary
while I was searching 'skewering,'
a method of putting rebels to death
by the Turks in Greece.
I was worried about Sumire's
sudden disappearance in Murakami's
*Sputnik Sweetheart*. Dropping the novel,
dropping the dictionary,
I am inside
my skull—
a living one's skull!
One day it will indistinguishably
roll among its kind
in our village cemetery.
It might so happen that
it will fall into the hands
of a black magician
who will perform secret rites
with it once it is midnight,
or it could become a begging bowl
of a fake mendicant
who will be frightening enough
to elicit alms
from my villagers.
Or if my fate is worse,
it will be still there
for the Cordelia of my daughter
to pick up blindfolded
and declare to the world,
it is her father's.
Will she still hear in it
the music of words
I rehearsed to myself

before I put them on paper,
or the susurrus of my desire
to leave them once and for all?
And my wife in her
visit to the village
on my quiet death anniversary
might stop in the cemetery,
facing my skull,.
and allow herself a wry smile,
musing, was sex in here,
as he claimed, not in the genitals?
And the worst would be,
holding it in her hands,
my mother would not believe
her son was so heavy. Instead,
she would resume talking
to herself: but my son's like
                    a bird who's always
        afloat in the wind.

## He Has in Him

He has in him a road, built over
the fields of paddy,
over the river, silted, buried,
over the temples razed,
over a pond of lilies.

He has abridged everything
from sunrise to sunset.
He has avoided mentors,
birds with clipped wings,
orgasms as disasters

and accepted all the perils
in building a road
like having to listen to the sound
of tyres on tar, the wailing
of the lilies, buried, in his sleep.

# Over a Cup of Tea

Our house is without a fence.
All that is there are only sparse hedges,
a few trees of jasmine and a *kaniar*
(of late I discovered this funnel
of a yellow flower is dear to our lord
Jagannath). Here sleep comes late
and leaves early. Still drowsy
you come out to the balcony
with the morning tea
and with an accumulation of
days of doing nothing. You imagine
the balance the days, emptied,
would make
were they to be placed
one atop another, and on top
of them all you sitting
with a cup of tea and letting
yourself flutter horizontally—
a 5′4″ temple banner.
Breaking the spell
a small grey bird comes hopping
towards you and picks worms
and seeds—the dawn is
so quiet you could hear them cracking
inside its beak. Then it goes away
without bothering to look at you,
making you realise the flimsiness,
the transparency of your being,
your being inconsequentially there
in one sunny morning with a
cup of tea, and your inability
to say something like
I let a morning with a bird go by
for sheer fear that the other bird
will soon be here somewhere
on electric wires or eucalyptus tops
with its too familiar note,

*tu tuu, tu tuu,*
which, in your mother tongue,
sounds like 'the end of you'.

## Moths

*"On Monday noon, 11•tribals were killed after police opened firing at a mob of oustees protesting the rehabilitation package handed over to them."*
— *The New Indian Express,* January 3, 2006, Bhubaneswar

Let me play a little innocuous game
keeping my children and wife away—
a game of fire.
A fire big enough
to consume moths.
Nobody else will be hurt;
only the moths.
I am said
to be stoking fire
but who else
is more adept
at self-immolation
than moths?
What is rumor
once moths, dismembered,
are cremated? What
trace in ash?
The fire I trust
with my fingers burnt.

## The Plight of Gods

They are here,
the Gods, in the images of clay
though just for a while.

They are here,
the poets with the feet
of bureaucrats.

They have their brand followers.
Kindly do not question
their loyalty,

for all you know
one even offered to dig out
one of his eyes to meet

the shortfall of one lotus
to make the one hundred and eight
for worship. (The followers

have always in them what one
might miss, otherwise.) Nothing
is as brief and as grand

as their existence, nothing
as sad as a bureaucrat's
retirement, nothing so

sad as the immersion
of Gods, sadder still
is the sight

of their straw limbs,
dismembered, afloat,
by the reeds in the ponds.

## Wall of Resistance

On damp walls
a pale yellow butterfly
caught in the web.

On the other side
water still overflowing,
those more, yet hard to ignore.

Fingers at the pen
snail-like;
don't they ever really move?

Hands jerk at the cold touch
of the table.
The obstinacy of wood

once it has taken shape.
What next? Moth? Ash?
Damp walls.

By now a spider
already upon its prey
and those snails

unmoving still
like your hand
cold in waiting upon a cold table.

## Sons and Fathers

Mahajanpur:
like any other village
where poor fathers are silenced
by their wealthy sons.

Fathers will be always poor to have set adrift
the paper boats of their sons
on the muddy currents of rain water
down the village roads.

Although the paper boats never return
(mostly, soon, they upturn)
the dream boat does,
loaded with the spices
of aromatic lands
and its sailors
belong to every other land but their own.

At the end of the village road
the tutelary deities, the mothers,
protecting their sons from the epidemics.
They have touched the horizons and,
in turn, sunk into the core.

Parentheses as they are,
they only embrace vast emptiness
among the sacred cows.

Mahajanpur,
memory locked
with a lone parent
or with parents separately lonely,

light years away
the paper boats with their dazed sailors
swirl in the deep, trying to strike
the shore they are forgetting.

## Anything Human is Proper

An excess of not doing anything—
sitting mud, with words upon deeds,
seeking the middle of nowhere.

The glare of those terrains
gaping like fatelines on palms.
Far away the woods tremble

and a deep cry emerges
to take shape, tinkering with the words.
Anything human is proper.

## Stalks of Lotus

It is ridiculous to raise a fence
around the steps, but that's it.
Raising a prayer from the graves
of lips or a flower from the bud
of a slit belief is how
it relates itself to life,
true or fictional. Admit,
in the fence you have a plinth
deeper than an azure despair.
You have made your steps auxiliary
with the gravels of slow hurt.
Each step, into bone's corridor.
Traces of light stale at each end
of the tunnel. What's dark
if it is seen, and life?
What is a fence if it is not
like a palm feeling for another
on the float of a last breath
that suddenly turns its face north
and blank, imparting to it the substance
of a lung to close upon
the night enveloping its lawn—
lotus stalks from the navel
of mud, or of a dwarfish god?

## What You Miss

All along it has been there.
You feel its presence
but could not be sure of the space
into which it empties itself.

It played with its shadow
till sundown. With the dark
it crept to your doorstep.
You felt its rustle but could not

touch it, sense its breath.
The walls you stared at
drew only a blank.
It sensed your despair

and dropped its quills.
Failing to get its hint
you sulk and then wilt.
Dawn is petals; dawn is quills.

THREE

# Malovika Pawar

**Malovika Pawar** has been a member of the Indian Administrative Service for the past 28 years. She holds a PhD in American literature from the US and an MSc in Social Policy from the London School of Economics. Her poems have appeared in *The Virginia Quarterly Review, The Western Humanities Review, Chndrabhaga* etc.

## And the Wolves are Circling the City

The terror of that Indian twilight!
The sun falling over the edge of the sugarcane fields,
crows dropping into trees.
Somewhere a peacock uttered its ragged cry.
In the geometric city, no cowbells
at *godhuli*, the hour of dust,
no smell of dust, no woodfires
to lull you home.
In the city, a catastrophe of twilight.
Dim lightbulbs flickered in dingy flats,
old men shuffled in verandas,
pressure-cookers whistled their deranged song
and TV sets gave forth their strident rant,
the evening news..

But the terror!
Something is falling down,
something is being pushed away,
day wrenched into night's maw,
something is sucking in the light,
something is dragging the world away.

Now wait for that other terror,
the terror of 4 a.m.,
when the wolves circle the city,
and some things must be admitted
to yourself.

## At A Resthouse, Near Jhansi

Circumspect, moon-white, an artifact of fear,
rooted in sinister country five miles out of Jhansi,
a resthouse, carelessly abandoned by the British.
By day, desolate grasses blew,
globed fruit dropped heavily to the ground;

by night, the aged caretaker with a beady squint
muttered to himself by a lantern's glow,
and the lights of Jhansi fluttered like forlorn flags
as distant as a dream from another life.

Stand by this decrepit railway track and marvel:
Could it be, behind those bland, secretive walls,
men wielded power, urged others
to treachery and death?
Fettered to these prosaic times, I fantasize
of British colonels calling out for drinks,
turning their clipped moustaches to the sun,
while their icy Memsahibs in watered silks
regally inspected flowers, dogs,
nurtured by men, whose language, whose lives,
they never would understand.

Post-partition baby, no witness to
the frenzy, the lashings, the flailings in the streets,
passionate curses spewing from the land,
I'm perfectly at liberty to cherish the romance:
Sundown on the terrace, shuttered verandas,
cool clean fingers twirling long-stemmed roses;
something that has eluded us so far.

The weight of the ineradicable past.

## Coming to Allahabad

Akbar *made Agra his capital and founded Illahabas, later called*
*Allahabad, near*
*ancient Prayaga.*

I
History flares in the nostrils of this city,
city of lepers , city of God,
of prayers and benedictions wasted

on the wind.
One saint, one fraud,
one politician that bayed like a hound,
one astrologer squinting at the skies,
one hunchback that walked the burning ghats..
All the way to the river, the wind
played the houses like an accordion,
and in these one-eyed houses,
those who had give up ,stammered
through their solitary lives,
and the whores , in desperation or lust
hiked up their petticoats
and taunted the men below.
The river trembled like a stealthy finger;
smell of woodsmoke, fragrance of sandalwood and incense.
Water lapped the stones in slow caress,
and marigold garlands drifted downstream.
A silence of cemeteries, of snow, of deserts
without name.

**II**

But opposite the ghats stands Akbạr's fort.
Another life bred on the hill above.
Memories of Mughals, trumpet and drum.
I want the caparisoned elephants of that age!
Bucklers and shields!
Dispatches from battle,
embroidered tales
of courtesans whose jingling feet elicited
showers of rupees,
of those two who played at chess while Lucknow fell,
of palanquins and musk,
of artistry,
of fear.

**III**

Oh, to have our small lives overtaken by pageantry!

My sticky passions smell as sweet
and rot as fast as marigolds in the stream.
May I be delivered from rectangular cities
full of palms,
sterility of choirboys, hotels that weep in bereavement ,
and fall into this chaos·
of heroes and leaning houses
streets as garrulous as old story-tellers
shaven-headed widows keening among the bones,
to fall into this pity,
to fall into this love,
to be rocked, violently ,
by time.

## In A Year of Burning, 1975

Just why do I scratch out these impotent words
deface such immaculately virginal paper?
Words are neither bread nor water
syllables do not give shelter.
Why then?

Outside my window an exploding India
cataclysms of nature, rape in the estuary
heavings and elemental sunderings of earth.
By a broken bridge on the Chambal they sit:
cattle and children; stonecutters; rib-thin, in the sand.

In the cities, hysteria in the streets;
men poised for suicide; in the slums, knives;
terror burning the flanks of the city
banners flung wetly down
slashed flags slapping on the hard pavement.

Think of all this tonight as you make that perfect serve
my worthy Galahad of the floodlit tennis court
while a savage India like a frenzied hound
leaps forward to assail your door
leaps.

# Expatriate Love

In an alien land, in a bleak and wet universe,
sleet drenching the streets, mud clogging the feet,
the pallid stars strung from an indefinite sky,
we meet.
In a garish town, in a circus of lost lovers,
under a tinsel tree.
Your mouth and your forehead are at war.
the one lashed with sensuality, tense
with thrashing thighs;
the other spoke of loincloth and sages
fasting in the hills, dry cacti, ascetic rage.
And then in the cloying cold, in rooms
wretched with rising damp,
you bring me a belly burning with vibrant tropic sun,
moist earth, monsoons, dripping pines,
you enclose me in a field of waving mustard,
you touch my hair with lone koel cries.
But when myths dry up, our childhood ends.
In the strange world outside, in the incomprehensible rain,
metal birds pecked at metal leaves,
the candlemakers fashioned their candles,
the grotesque continued to grin,
cannibals walked through London town,
flesh was riveted to flesh, flesh was torn from flesh,
the one-eyed children dawdled in the parks.
Expatriates both from that old country
we flung away with curses
and this wonderful monster land we chose,
mouth on mouth we lie, thigh on thigh,
while a continent away, as vengeful tigers
leap from bamboo grass, and pavements explode in flames
dark-eyed children with stones in their hands
knock at our dreams and will not let us sleep.

# By the Ghaggar River Terraces, near Pinjore

This is a river of many alluvial secrets.
She surprises; stuns by swift attack;
is meditative by day, cruel at night.

**1**

In April, the Ghaggar lay supine,
face averted like a disinterested lover's,
its stance anemic, its bed the colour of slate,
its terraces the occasional haunt of mountain hawk and eagle.
On either bank, tentative and restless land,
alternately embraced and discarded by the river.
And north of the river, the young Himalayas
rose from the plains with brutal suddenness.

In April, torpor glazed this landscape.
Then, known in August, lashed by wet winds,
the river reared on its hind legs
and gave its lion–roar, thundered in the valleys, clutched at its banks,
crushed huts, devoured them, ate roads and bridges,
engendered streams.
Earth felt desirable again.

**2**

All sensations are purer in the hills.
If fear, then it is a terror so intense
that the flapping of a raven's wing
or the distant rumble of a falling rock

hisses like a snake at one's ribs.
And in my other life, buried in the plains below, there were lovers, slammed doors,
irrevocable journeys, taxis taken and paid for,
strangled farewells at airports.
All hushed, all swept away, all
finished, all obliterated, in the silence
of this geological hour.

**3**

In the spring when the gulmohar was sprinkled
like blood over the forest,
the villagers crept to the river and cried out:
"Ghaggar, ma, mother, protectress of hill-folk,
sister to Bhagirathi,
spawned in the same grottoes,
swelling from the same ice,
let your roars lull us,
let us lie on your boulders,
wash us with your milk."

And all afternoon, while great
hieratic birds wheeled in an empty sky,
the small flowers dropped into the
easy waters
of this river,

that eats trees, destinies.

# FOUR

# Soni Wadhwa

**Soni Wadhwa** is a research scholar in Literature Studies. She has been teaching papers on Mass Media in different colleges in Mumbai. Her research interests are Sindhi Studies, Literary and Cultural Theory, Cultural Studies and Spatial Criticism. She lives in Mumbai.

## Repulsion

I burst the pebbles in my mother's eyes.
Picking the crushed powder like a pinch of salt,
They revel in the orgy of sound,
When they curse.
In this dark
A man smells of a eunuch and
A eunuch smells of a man
(May I undo what I have done?)
With a stony touch that strangulates,
Drags a fish out of the water
And laughs while it dangles
The bats mourn and howl.

## Earth

When last the tree danced,
My child patronized it by smiling.
Both of them make a ball of each other.
As if some clay is condensed with moonlight.

The clay that every nose longs for
That gives shelter,
That contains the dead,
That feeds the hungry mouths,
Bequeathed to the living.

Krishna, is there nothing else to eat?
It is not at all filling.
Impoverishing thousands of children day by day.

## The Body Series

With a sober swinging nose
The inhaled air caused an outburst.
The eyes exploded out of sockets.
The.hunger so hungry that it ate up hunger.
The soul that is pushed in
With a palm dashing against the cleavage,
Becomes a misfit, doesn't it?
The boozing mind drowned in the mouth.
The hands want to sway in ecstasy.
The hands want to sway in ecstasy.
They set the trunk ablaze.
The fire chains it suffocating the ankles.

## Couple(t)s

The couplet is so calculated.
Calculated beauty in fixed rhythm
Made to rhyme
Anticipating its ends
Climbing towards the apex of limited choices.
At least, it narrows down your options.
One great controlled beauty
Of its earlier tunes
Drowns into banging
And tires the jaw.
The rest is not silence
Deafness follows.
Death follows.
Two deaths so intertwined
That their souls are cut into halves by the chain that bound
their feet
They continue to live like Siamese twins.

# Feminism/Poetry

### One

Let's read theory and laugh,
It is a laughing gas.
Let's explore the holes of out bodies
With our fingers.
What has theory done to us?
We have begun to like poetry!
And the blank space around its lines
Overflows to gape at us.
The silence of the white blankness
Screams more than black words.
The rest is not silence.
Theory reminds us that
While the whole body is
Vulnerable to kisses and licks,
The soles of my feet are still virgin.

### Two

When god jumped on earth
To live life created by him
People were staring at him for his bad manners.
He was washing his hands in my balcony.
I warned him,
"You will next begin to blow your nose here,
Control yourself."
He did not listen and I broke his nose.
He cried, it was his life,
It was his nose. And he did what every man does
To avenge an insult. I was again
Lecturing him.
He said, "You are just another fucking feminist"
Others admire him for his humility, sincerity,
Honesty and all that.
I don't know, why I see every great man
As just another misogynist.

**Three**

My words fly for someone miles away.
He examines them privately as if he is
Wrapped in them as if they are a skirt.
I construct my stanzas as two long legs-
Stainless, soft, smooth. But all he can see is
That I stink between my legs.
I cannot pat my man-poet. Poetry cannot convey
The physics of life. He says,
"Why are we wasting out time, babe?
Poetry is a small whistle. Do not push air
So forcefully. Your breasts are incapable delicate"

**Four**

He: I love your long hair
She: Of course, you do. It is a sign of patriarchy.
He: You smell of...
She: I know, of a Xeroxed paper.
He: Your body...
She: Oh yes, it farts often. Come on, say it.
He: You are very intelligent.
She: Yeah! I know I am not beautiful.
He: But...lesdilashquoprinesquitamdi-
She: That's OK. I know you love me. Don't bother about words.

## On Walking

Walking is a dream
Slitting across eons of space
At a hai-hai speed.
When I walk, I leap out of myself
To catch up with God,
To help him serve humanity
And other trespassers.
Walking is making love to the road
When it sends shivers up the spine.
Walking is meditating and sleeping in the air.

# On Watching Memories

Darling, I remember the day
You first came home wet with first rain
Wet with dark smell of your
Body, water, and wet mud.
Your drenched blue shirt clung to your body
Biting the hell out of your body hair
Leaving it awake and aroused,
Fresh, gleaming in the last lees of water.
You stood there struggling with your clothes.
Saving our furniture at the same time.
A shower, you thought, would refresh you.
But I saw two layers of waters sliding
Your body, helping each other
Stick to you.
And you thought something was wrong
With the towel.
And I envied both the waters and the towel.
Somehow, the scene does not leave
My mind.
It remains there like set in a perfect gaze
Centering on you.

# FIVE
# Rumjhum Biswas

**Rumjhum Biswas's** poetry and fiction have been published in India and abroad. One of her poems was long listed in the Bridport Poetry Prize 2006 and was also a finalist in the 2010 Aesthetica Creative Arts Contest. She has won prizes in poetry contests in India and her work has been commended abroad. She is also a Puchcart nominee. She has participated in poetry and literary festivals in Chennai and Hyderabad.

## Hardwar

The woman pours mug after mug
of water that still mirrors
the clarity of icy mountains gushing innocently down
into this sage town of gridlocked piety.

Her heaving chest cries out
for the clinging sari to be shed as she plunges
in believing all her sins, even her supposed sins
that no one else knows of, will be cleansed.

Her gasps, yelps and rolling eyes, every time
the water stings her flesh into fresh awareness embarrasses
the man beside her as he clasps her elbow. His eyes
show concern; excitement engorges his crotch.

Further away, on the concrete bank
snakes cling to bony shanks
or rest in baskets, shoulders and laps.
Tender coils of ornamental fangs

chaffing against holy beads, they receive
inedible flowers, fruits, *salaams* of believers
and the fear of tourists, but the coins
are scarcer nowadays. Still further down

an arrogant cow brushes her way past
the slower moving bipeds. She has no time
for you if you don't have an offering
in your hand. And, mother far, far away

in her much ornamented prayer room
along with all the grandmothers and
widowed aunts from your suddenly
very extensive family - all those

who had commissioned you to bring back these

sin-washing waters in jam jars and discarded
plastic bottles as they prayed - they are the ones
with boundless faith, believing you to be twice blessed.

## Small Town Road One Night

A child's laughter hurtles through the dark
like a puppy with a stolen bone. I am quite alone.
The sulky stare of a street lamp, stubbornly hugging
the grassy edge of this narrow small town road
slithering ahead of me;
this black tar road, this solitary lamp,
this backdrop of blacker-still night.
The squawk of an errant egret returning
to its nest long past curfew hour. White wings
rowing through sky - a blur
of anxious white, a flustered ghost in the moist black night.

No one can claim my space here, but who
do I really need? The cities are mixed-fruit jam jars.
Blended, you can be still so alone. That solitude is terrible.
You are squeezed in like that extra shred of underwear
into a box bursting at the seams. You are slung
neck to neck with people bearing grim,
no-trespassing signs for faces.

Now, my small town road is different. It
murmurs its own stories as it unwinds.
I am welcome to listen if I want, nobody invites.
I am free to lend an ear. It is alright
to eavesdrop. I may talk
to myself, if I so choose and my road will listen.
My monologue will not be an eccentric's soliloquy. Perhaps
a gecko below a loose brick in a dark garden wall
will chuck-chuck out of sympathy, or a shrew
scuttling busily will squeak her disapproval. It is all right.

They don't mind. Just as I don't mind that child's laughter
hurtling towards me in the dark,
nuzzling its way into my ear, seeking
a soft warm hole to bury its bone.

## Desecration

The *Rakta Karabi* blooms in blood red defiance.
Stupefying my neighbor's patch of pious flowers.
A pristine gray sky tilts with its load of secrets. But
no cloud splits apart. And, man does not yield

In this tug-of-war between nature and man
rivers in their rage whip off the clothes of fish,
cruelly making them thresh for shame
in the mud. There is no one to protest
their molested dignity. There is no one
to protect my neighbor's flowers.

But the Rakta Karabi blossoms have defied
protection. They have already
accepted their fate. And they have
let out their blood to pierce the sky.

Each blossom protruding like the violated parting
of a pre-pubescent virgin's thighs.

Note: *Karabi* is the Bengali word for Oleander; *Rakta* means blood in Bengali; the oleander flowers here are of the blood red variety.

## Monday Aubade

A strangled anthem croaks.
The words wrung
out from its twisted throat,
the tune trickling

down like a thin
ruby red snake
of blood from a burst vein.

What agony is this in the morning?

A chorus of children.
Their hearts and feet bared
to the elements. Their tired
sleep and pay deprived school master.
His broken harmonium
and bladder full
of passed-out desires
and passed over dreams.

But patriotism will prevail.
At least, as a good example.
Just as much as children
will be disciplined with hunger.

So it happens.

The school bell tolls.
The Anthem's head rolls.
Another dirge heralds another Monday.

## Morning Encounter

Suddenly here
on my everyday walk
in the park by the beach
of familiar things – a familiar spring
of flowers and grass, sky and trees
and some friendly faces - it lies
bang in the centre of my path.

Not your everyday garden variety. It is

one that tenderly
uncoils its length of glistening sinew.
My walk is refreshed by this unfamiliar facet;
made more brilliant and more rare
than the King Cobra's mythical gem.

My walk which was never the drudgery
of an everyday chore,
now moment by moment more
mysterious grows.
Renewing me like the sloughing off
of old skin. Discarding the chilblains
of an unreasonably cold season.

I who had hitherto only known
the unearthing of mounds,
the soft soil pills of blind wriggly things
with their hearts beating softly in the earth,
now inhale a sharp sensation
and catch
a stillness in my veins.
I soak up a sudden sunlit shaft.
I tether my larking heart.
I make my senses more acute.
For here before me on this everyday path
by the beach is this
geometric rhythm of light cutting
into the serpent's diamond gaze.

**Poet's note:** In Bengali myth and folklore serpents have a gem on their hoods, which were sought after by princes and sorcerers alike, and figure in many Bengali folk and fairy tales.

## My Heart has Grown Small

My heart has grown small
this much I can tell you
I do not ask your forgiveness
what's the use of explaining

my heart has no more space
for all those things –
ideals, places, people
even the desire for certain favorite foods
is gone
you raise your eye brows
surprised to see me chomp on chilies
red and green with a lethal bite
my eyes no longer water
my tongue runs over my palate
tasting and re-tasting the fire
perhaps you remember the girl
who used to cry easily
the girl who embraced every iota
crumb of love thrown her way
but I tell you now
my heart has grown small
it no longer has
the large open spaces
the airy rooms that used to expand
no matter how much
you stuffed it
my heart has grown small
it can only peck at tidbits
of ideals, places, people
it can only love the chosen few
in fits and starts, in hurried gulps
you will only torture yourself
by remembering
you will make yourself miserable
why don't you try to love me
a little less? It would make things
so much easier for me, for both
of us. My heart
has grown small
It can no longer carry
the full weight of your love.

# Nostalgia

*(Remembering Diwali in the Home Country)*

Autumn is a wafting memory in my heart
now that the Sun has begun to sulk
complaining that the sky is too small.
His otherwise fiery mane droops
as he licks his wounds. Bides his time
But soon his mane will elongate,
the power will surge down his flanks.
Right now though, this narrow blue strip is his beat.

But what about those who left the dried leaves
of the Frangipani tree between the brittle pages
of long unturned poetry books
and sat listening to English Pop over the radio,
meticulously copying into longhand
lyrics without accents on brightly collaged scrapbooks?

During afternoons of sleepy flies, fish and rice
and betel nuts quietly splitting. Of quilts laid out
to soak the sun alongside pickles spread
on kite and gossip festooned terraces. When you
endeavored to gather what heat you could. And
old wool was refreshed between wrists and knees,
the fragrance of melted beeswax revisited
in foil cups. The honeyed air hummed
with the cooking of sweetmeats. And age old
ghost stories were dressed anew...

What about them? Ah yes. What about it then?
When you know in your bones
that those were just some of the unimportant things
from the life you left behind, and in which
tradition perhaps still lives.
In which memory still whirrs like a humming bird,
even though it knows
that nostalgia is after all a tricky hive of bees.

## Rapture of the Deep

The umbra of your soul
becomes blue here

where centuries of icy restraint
are converted

into popsicle bright, indigo lush layers
of incomprehensible beauty

You begin to spiral through translucent
filaments of questions - Why

did the dreamer's dream start to turn and elongate
into the bluebird's song? When

did the artist crush cerulean with marble mortar
to pollinate the waters? How

did the weight of Beryline tunnel through teal with a speed of
purpose
more potent than a chalice dipped into Lethe? Can anything

be as quiet as the shades that haunt
the silences of this watery world?

We derive so much of succor from the cobalt dish of sky
gently pouring into oceans, lakes and rivers. Yet,

sailors dread that deep dive where azure and ultramarine lie
counting time on ocean washed spherules

swept aside by the webbed and finned,
the fronded and plumed mysteries.

Everything is stilled by the deep
singing a certain unspoken song

of such soul numbing beauty
that you cannot, you must not, and you do not

even try to return to your harsh world
of unquiet colour

## Road Map

Life takes you by the scruff of your neck
and makes you face the circus mirrors.
Concave, convex, crooked walls of parody
where beauty is beastified. Truth defied
Defiled. And Ridicule rebounds
from wall to polished wall,

where will you run if you stay indoors?
Who was there beside you, when
you slipped out
from your mother's wounded womb?
Who will be there
beside you, on the smoking pyre?

When you were given a voice, you
were given a task, your duty
on the line of fire.
you were given no rights
to shirk and run, dig a trench.
You were given a gun.
Not to defend or offend, but
to release the bullets to find their own mark.

What is a snigger, but a silly sound.
What is a smirk, but a paltry picture.
Are these the ants and flies
that are making you cry?

The Nazis could not crush
the voice of a thirteen year old child.

## The Other Side of the Sun

Dusk has hefted this bloodless day
upon grim shoulders
and is now striding towards a horizon
where the Borealis are waiting
to feed...

Night drops down on iron haunches
and scans the sky
for a Moon, any Moon. Even an Arabian Moon.
Instead this night is hit full in the face
with wind, sleet and hail

Snarling at this January day, winter's dragon
teeth stand
row by row by row on power lines and telephone poles,
ready to champ down hard
on bird, beast and man...

Its power is elusive. Elusive like the mirages
in the burning fields
on the other side of the sun. Redemption is too far away
and winter's flinty fingers are breaking now
over the dreams of the dead lying forgotten
in unimportant lands.

# SIX
# Sudeep Sen

**Sudeep Sen** has published a dozen book including *Postmarked India: New & Selected Poems* (HarperCollins), and *The HarperCollins Book of English Poetry* (editor). His poems have been translated into twenty-five languages. His words have appeared in the *TLS, Newsweek, Guardian, Observer, Independent, Telegraph, Herald, Harvard Review, Hindu, Hindustan Times, Times of India, Outlook, India Today*. He is the editorial director of AARK ARTS and the editor of *Atlas*.

# Mediterranean

**1**

A bright red boat
Yellow capsicums

Blue fishing nets
Ochre fort walls

**2**

Sahar's silk blouse
gold and sheer

Her dark black
*kohl*-lined lashes

**3**

A street child's
brown fists

holding the rainbow
in his small grasp

**4**

My lost memory
white and frozen

now melts colour
ready to refract

# Offering

the kindness of libation, lyric, and blood

her endless notes left for me—
little secrets, graces—
trills recorded on blue and purple parchment
to be lipped, tasted, devoured—

only essence remains—
its stickiness, its juice, its memory

seamless juxtaposition—
the brute and the passion,
dry of the bone and wet of the sea,
coarseness of the page and smooth of the nib's iridium

I try and trace a line, a very long line—

the ink blots
as this line's linear edge
dissolves and frays —

like capillary threads
gone mad
twirling in the deep heat of the tropics—

threads unravelling,
each sinew tense with the want of moisture
and the other's flesh

there are no endings here—
only beginnings—
precious incipience—

translucent drops of sweat
perched precariously on her collar-bone
waiting to slide,

roll unannounced into the gulleys
that yearn to soak in the rain—

heart-beat shift
the shape of globules
as they alter their balance and colour,
changing their very point of gravity—

constantly deceiving the other

I stand, wanting—
wanting more of the bone's dry edge,
the infinite blur of desire,
the dream,
the wet, the salt, the ink,
and the underside of her skin

## Bharatanatyam Dancer

*for Leela Samson*

Spaces in the electric air divide themselves
in circular rhythms, as the slender
grace of your arms and bell-tied ankles
describe a geometric topography, real, cosmic,
one that once reverberated continually in
a prescribed courtyard of an ancient temple

in South India. As your eyelids flit and flirt, and
match the subtle *abhinaya* in a flutter
of eye-lashes, the pupils create an
unusual focus, sight only ciliary muscles
blessed and cloaked in celestial *kaajal*
could possibly enact.

The raw brightness of *kanjeevaram* silk, of
your breath, and the nobility of antique silver
adorns you and your dance, reminding us of

the treasure chest that is only
half-exposed, disclosed just enough, barely —
for art in its purest form never reveals all.

Even after the arc lights have long faded,
the audience, now invisible, have stayed over.
Here, I can still see your pirouettes, frozen
as time-lapse exposures, feel
the murmuring shadow of an accompanist's
intricate *raga* in this theatre of darkness,

a darkness where oblique memories of my
quiet Kalakshetra days filter,
matching your very own of another time,
where darkness itself is sleeping light,
light that merges, reshapes, and ignites,
dancing delicately in the half-light.

But it is this sacred darkness that endures,
melting light with desire, desire that simmers
and sparks the radiance of your
quiet femininity, as the female dancer
now illuminates everything visible: clear,
poetic, passionate, and ice-pure.

Note: The line-end rhyme-scheme — a b a c c a ... d b d e e d ... f b f g g f ... — maps and mirrors the actual classical dance step-pattern and beat — ta dhin ta thaye thaye ta. Left-hand margin indentations match the same scheme and form.

## Choice

*drawing a breath between each*
*sentence, trailing closely every word.*
— JAMES HOCH, 'Draft' in *Miscreants*

**1.**

*some things, I knew,*
*were beyond choosing:*

didu — grandmother — wilting
under cancer's terminus care —

mama's mysterious disappearance —
ventilator vibrating, severed
silently, in the hospital's unkempt dark —

an old friend's biting silence — unexplained —
promised loyalties melting for profit
abandoning long familial presences of
trust —

devi's jealous heart misreading emails
hacked carefully under cover,
her fingernails ripping
unformed poems, bloodied, scarred —
my diary pages weeping wordlessly —
my children aborted, my poetry breathless forever.

2.

these are acts that enact themselves, regardless —
helpless, as I am,
torn asunder permanently, drugged, numbed.

strange love, this is — *a salving:*
*what medics and nurses do.*

i live buddha-like, unblinking, a painted vacant smile —
one that stores pain and painlessness —
someone else's nirvana thrust upon me.

*some things I* once believed in
are *beyond* my *choosing* —
choosing is a choice unavailable to me.

## Flying Home

I meticulously stitch time through the embroidered sky,
 through its unpredictable lumps and hollows. I

am going home once again from another
 home, escaping the weave of reality into another

one, one that gently reminds and stalls
 to confirm: my body is the step-son of my soul.

But what talk of soul and skin
 in this day and age, such ephemeral things

that cross-weaves blood and breath
 into clotted zones of true escape.

What talk of flight time and flying
 when real flights of fancy are crying

to stay buoyant unpredictably in mid-air
 amid pain, peace, and belief: just like thin air

sketches, where another home is built
 in free space vacuum, as another patchwork quilt

is quietly wrapped around, gently, in memoriam.

## Kargil

Ten years on, I came searching for
          war signs of the past
expecting remnants — magazine debris,
unexploded shells,
     shrapnel
          that mark bomb wounds.

I came looking for
ghosts —
people past, skeletons charred,
abandoned
brick-wood-cement
that once housed them.

I could only find whispers —
whispers among the clamour
of a small town outpost
in full throttle —
everyday chores
sketching outward signs
of normality and life.

In that bustle
I spot war-lines of a decade ago —
though the storylines
are kept buried, wrapped
in old newsprint.

There is order amid uneasiness —
the muezzin's cry,
the monk's chant —
baritones
merging in their separateness.

At the bus station
black coughs of exhaust
smoke-screens everything.
The roads meet
and after the crossroad ritual
diverge,
skating along the undotted lines
of control.
A porous garland
with cracked beads
adorns Tiger Hill.
Beyond the mountains

are dark memories,
and beyond them
no one knows,
and beyond them
no one wants to know.

Even the flight of birds
that wing over their crests
don't know which feathers to down.
Chameleon-like
they fly, tracing perfect parabolas.

I look up
and calculate their exact arc
and find instead, a flawed theorem.

## Eating Guavas Outside Taj Mahal

for Kwame Dawes

*The heavy drunken aroma*
*of fresh guavas*
is too sweet for me to bear.

Instead, I drink its nectar
not as liquid-pulp
but as raw unsmooth fruit.

I bite its light-green rough skin
the way I used to
approach a sugarcane stalk

as a child
crunching every fibre
to extract their juice.

There are memories —
memories attached to food
and their consumption.

There are memories
  about the rituals of intake —
how certain foods

are allowed or disallowed
  depending on God's stance
and their place

in the lofty hierarchies
  they create.
How misplaced these stations

are — God, Emperor, Man
  all mistaken — proud errors
of selfhood, status, and ego.

Even under prayer's veil,
  there is something about
eating guavas with unwashed

hands, tasting its taste before
  *masala,* lemon and rock-salt
turn them into sprightly salad —

seed's bone-crack intentions
  slip, cloaked —
buried before they fruit.

SEVEN

# Nabanita Kanungo

**Nabanita Kanungo** was born in Shillong, Meghalaya, 1981. She completed her MA in Geography from the North-Eastern Hill University and is currently pursuing her PhD in the subject. Her poems have appeared in *Indian Literature* and *Muse India.*

## A Road

The swig of the countryside
will gather as a tear,
the last tree will make home of my eyes,
the passing rock, replace my heart.

Back in the city,
too much time sits on a chair beside a window.
I struggle to see my ripening in berries,
my yellowing in a leaf
and commit juvenile burdens
to a soft folder;

afternoons
of laughing with friends
and marveling at firs,

puffs
of smoke from the village's own pipe
and the return to statutory warnings,

glimpses
of a man sleeping on grass
and grass sleeping on him.

The road plunges on,
surges past,
much later
with all its hill-sides,
and ravines
painfully clear,
with the same amount of light and rain

and the wind is still felt
intimately on the fingers
as I carry it
across places

far and grey,
in slow-moving clips
that emphasize how a fern was unmindfully plucked
and stored in a book,

how openings and closings
are always
in perspective,
a road.

## I Was Born

Somewhere, in the meshes of horror,
a seed was spilt. I was born.
I was inscribed in the maps that
went to the North East Frontier Agency with my grandfather,
stashed in his brief-case-skull, it's being of a clerk,
it's honest earnings
at the time of the Naga uprising;
I was the semi-conscious ash of his stolen hearth.

I was born in my father's difficult birth;
Habiganj was where he kicked himself to life,
as the mid-wife stifled his mother's cries
so that the rioters wouldn't hear.

I was born underneath the feet of a woman
who saw her son being hacked alive
before she was hanged naked to a *palash* tree,
and then burnt.

I was there in that time, in pelted stones
and the earthen eyes that froze, oozing dreams,
the pots that bubbled with aid,
camps where life was bought with the last gold.

Still later, I was born in a hill
where the landscape offered alms;

the refuge of delusion.
I was the red-soil where faces fell
and feet stumbled at the gain of memory,
each day, each moment.

I was born in lost businesses,
and talents that grew legs to run away
into the ever-distant markets of favor.
I was born in this need to re-figure everything one has
on geography's leathery skin, history's long tongue.

And all the time, there was a difference
of being born in the throes of being up-rooted,
like the event of a wild beast
being transferred to a sanctuary and then a zoo.
But the sameness of it is an insanity killing slowly,
an acceptance that bids me want to be born again
in a snake-hole or a rabbit's burrow.

## Mylliem Now

When......if
nascent pines run their fingers on your grassy skin
and the winds leave fern-like earrings
tinkling under your craggy ears
Mylliem, remember me.
Remember how I had seen your rain,
its portion of leaf and moss
erupting like an august lava
from fissures of your heart,
how eagerly I had grabbed a handful of it
to scatter on thought's sterile ground;
small green sparks
in a grey square of hollows.
You tattooed your passion
through the hands of a blacksmith,
on a sheet of his metallic life;
I heard you.

I hear you now as well
in the rain of anvil and hammer;
it imitates you doing similar things
to cabbage and potato- patterned slopes.

I stood smiling
by what looked like half eaten cakes
only you cried and told me
they were hills;
chunks shorn of soil's ferric-red joy.
You said I must speak to trees;
know them before I left,
those delirious roots and trunks
that barely stood half gripping their sliced assurance.
I met precocious rivers
pregnant with early silt.
Soon, your regimes will reveal
squalid convexes of an embryonic town,
concrete on your fringes,
impending steel in the resolute years,
pushing open like the jaws of a vice.

Is nativity so bad?
Mylliem, freeze or you'll die.
And remember me.
For I have walked mental maps of sorrow's hills
and dusks have always led me
to that deliberate practice—
regurgitating textures,
feeling the likes of you on my worsted tongue,
chewing a fading cud of impressions,
some childhood sketchpen-perfect greens.

## Her Thighs Still Smell of Milk

The woman who walked past her home,
with expectations in her womb,

returned elsewhere with a pail of trials.
Her steps must have fallen softly
on leaves once red with youth
for now they are a blazing canopy
of yellow addresses and compensations,
written in an awkward hand
on the other side of a divided sky.
She must have stopped short
to gain breath at the corner
where trees and everything turn black
against a dying sun.
Those silhouettes she must have passed,
settling the dust raised on streets, late noons;
dousing fire with the swell of tides,
until they stopped spilling from age's curve,
the container at her hip.
Her Krishna must have travelled to that distant haze,
on her lips;
he outlived her in a song cast through evenings.

Her thighs still smell of milk
and her bosom, of blood.
Why do I want to dredge the music
out of her fluids?
Now when she has seeped down
the stony cracks of my story
with a limp map half-flying
from a shock-stiffened hand,
waiting for the last ceremonial rite
my memory can afford.

For when they killed her at the border
a child was still tugging at her dead nipple.

## Native Man

The plum squirts joy from your simple heart.
Late into the year,

a small patch of your winter's sun,
kneads my cold spine,
bakes a hum.
Then, I trace your steps on terraces of rice
that ascend from the loam of my lost homeland.

Swan, you slice my lake of memories.
Your amethyst name is the pen
that unlocks the rain-laden story of my eyes,
a warm wind that rises on the monsoon's wheel
to churn my ink, my night.

I grow from a mossy knot
in the tall spires of your pines.
I rest my sorrow on the place
where the rough branch forks from your shoulders
and carves the wooden-cross.

Native man, lull me with wounds if not sons,
I will play with the daughter you cannot give.
Yet, your eternal self will find me
waiting for the seed of words,
the stones in your eyes.

Wet grass on wandering feet,
your hands of the cave's milk,
give your rain upon the path of my thirst.

## Rain

To the roof's tin-song,
the wild dance of leaves,
to the aroma of fried needs
to innocent things that died on me
and killed me innocently.....
The ode capsizes
like a naive paper-boat,
and a marooned day slants its gaze
to spot the rainbow flowing on playful streets.

Towards the evening,
I grow inward-looking
and think of lost friends and verses.

Some anger hurls my words into a hiss.
The old lament of time.

Now a bruise appears as the sky,
and a million tongues descend
to lick the solitary hour.

## The Missing Tooth

There were reasons for which we had it painfully uprooted
and now the gap of the missing tooth
is an embarrassing memory in the mouth.

But the tongue is a child,
habitually searching for a world
where it is not.

## The Protagonists

Who were we?
Honchos of grief,
bartering the laws of life for a smile,
shamelessly weaving pine leaves into hidden shapes and secrets.

We did not lick the sun
or kiss the moon.
There were no stars to pluck from night's canopy.

With a longing as our only belonging,
we carried a bundle to the forest of tastes;
those simple adventures that left me orange-squash-thirsty

and drove you to collect rainbow-colored skies on your tongue.

We must have mistaken an amphitheatre for hills
and bunches of pointed fingers for orchids.

Did you feel the same way as I did when we froze?
Did you hear the background petrify,
the sound of something cracking between us?

I do not know how a roll of small names began ascending from our feet.
I do not know who arranged us in the order of appearance.

## Give the Winds a Clue

**I**

Give the winds a clue
as to where the moon has sprinkled our silver memoirs.

I can swear I heard an antique creak, a crying child,
the rustle of wet rice like secrets fuming
in clichéd metal boxes.

Agreement papers, slip-shod transactions,
no agreement, no transaction,
all running the pavilion in haste;
hazards and the hope of life's benefit of doubt.

These split moments are twanging from some mother's hair
like the remains of a curled ribbon of bamboo and cane,
as old Benarasi sarees are re-sewn
with stars torn from a Shillong night.

Some grandmothers
who bottled the summers of their tamarind youth
and who could have pickled Sylhet
if they had the sun and some time.

Pack your goats and children and leave.
The coordinates have changed.

**II**

Confused houses do not shelter.
I have not the fire to love the roof of nowhere.
The asbestos of my context has a leak of pain
and it would rhyme if I said
that here, joy flows in like acid-rain.

The pigeon is better off or the crow.
I have become a poet,
a mind, a map,
anything that does not boast of a liver

For, I grew up in a concrete 'where'
of the orchid and the *khtung*
perhaps in a hollow of rain-washed lime-stone,
away from axes and saws and the stories they made
pinning a whole tree with women's breasts.
The old lady who sells oranges
and gave me one for free one day,
haunts my fugitive dreams
and I have pictures of her son
who laid a flower on my charred lips.

## A Bend in Time

I do not suckle hopes anymore.
Only a tired poem finds my breasts at night.

I must have been to that cubicle again
where the road takes a bend in time
to hide lovers escaping their eternal pain,
and it rains forever.

I have brought home a familiar smell—
some June and you in my clothes.

## Citizenship

This writing into winding ways,
is a habit now,
encoding a terrible fear in a poem:

An evening opens suddenly
brazen like an antonym
with wailings of a bitter kite hanging from a tree,
the doom of wings on the electric pole,
and reminds that the unfortunate event of being here
is but to flap unto the sure silence ahead.

I could not go protest-marching anywhere
except behind a curtain;
there, I folded my rights, even wind.
I muted pain's language with my alienness,
and it stayed in my eyes,
at times like meals suspended in the horizon,
two crumbs of decent life
and at others, like abscessed dreams
of earning a house.

The capture weighs down,
nostalgia's cloud-coloured guilt
heavy with landscapes of my scattered biography,
and a cottage that fits neatly in the region of rain.
And I do not even raise my head so much
as to stitch the holes in my tent.
I apologise for these stars.
They are fake,
like my citizenship.
But the night is not spurious;
always a dark, genuine precipitate
that becomes of looking,
of loving the hills
and not the distant corporation of success
and will only proceed from one page upon another
in search of belongingness;

an ink, that however deep,
does not turn a space into a place.

# EIGHT
# Yuyutsu Sharma

Recipient of fellowships and grants from The Rockefeller Foundation and Ireland Literature Exchange, Punjab born and Kathmandu-based poet, **Yuyutsu Sharma** has published nine poetry collections including, *Milarepa's Bones, Helambu, Space Cake, Amsterdam, Annapurna Poems,* and *www.nepal-trilogy.de*. Yuyutsu's works have appeared in *Poetry Review, Chanrdrabhaga, Sodobnost, Amsterdam Weekly, Indian Literature, Irish Pages, Delo, Omega, Exiled Ink, Iton77, The Little Magazine, The Telegraph, Indian Express* and *Asiaweek*. His poetry has been translated into German, French, Italian, Slovenian, Hebrew, Spanish and Dutch. Half the year, he travels and reads all over the world but goes trekking in the Himalayas when back home.

## Sherpa Woman

Toothless Sherpa mother
let me sleep

deepest sleep
of my life

in her warm
doorless barn

lighted by moonlight
filtering through

the fractures
of her wooden walls.

## Mules

On the great Tibetan
salt route they meet me again

old forsaken friends ...

On their faces
fatigue of a drunken sleep

their lives worn out,
their legs twisted, shaking

from carrying
illustrious flags of bleeding ascents.

Age long bells clinging
to them like festering wounds

beating notes
of a slavery modernism brings:

cartons of Iceberg, mineral water bottles,
solar heaters, Chinese tiles, tin cans, carom boards

sacks of rice
and iodized salt from the plains of Nepal Terai.

Butterflies of
the terraced fields know their names.

Singing brooks tempests
of their breathless climbs.

Traffic alert
and time-tested, they climb

carrying
dreams of posh peacocks

pamphlets
of a secret religious war

filth
of an ecologist's sterile semen

entire kitchen
for a cocktail party at the base camp

defunct development
agenda of guilty donors

the West's weird visions
lusting for an instant purge.

Stone steps
of the mountains embossed

on their drugged brains,
like lines of aborted love

scratched
on the historic rocks of waterspouts.

Starry skies
of the dozing valleys know

the ache
of their secret sweat.

Sunny days
along the crystal rivers

taste
of their bleeding eyes.

Greatest fiction
of the struggling lives lost,

like real mules
clattering their hooves on the flagstones,

in circling
the cruel grandeur

of blood thirsty
mule paths around the glaciers of Annapurnas.

## Little Paradise Lodge

My pen frozen against
the daggers of Annapurnas...

On an oblong shapeless plank chopped
from a sandal wood tree trunk and used as a table

I place my elbows
and hold my face in my hands.

Blinding snows of the Annapurna Ridge,
Hyunchali, shining in the eye of my mind,

I sit in the spacious courtyard of your paradise lodge,
deciphering the shrill notes of birds in the mossy trees.

One bird initiates a lilting note
like our meeting while
other lets loose a racket of breath-whistles
ending with question tags—
Can I stay longer, at least one more day,
in your little paradise lodge?

Two birds playing in the crimson cherry tree
stir a chord that seems
like opening up of the blossoms
of our bodies—Would you take me away and marry me?

But what about the electric whistle,
this cicada's constant chirr,
the struggle of our breathless bodies
against dark soot of the night?

The pigeons strutting freely in your courtyard
coo like exhausted porters
climbing the mule paths in the singing gorges.
Their guttural quataquatantankua—
they seem to be using human language,
a kind of hushed speech that robbers might use.

Love, in the courtyard of your little paradise lodge
I see the silence turning flowers into daggers

A herd of cows shuffles past me in a joyous mood
festive like young girls going to a hillside fair
saying — Don't go away, Dai, we would be back
until dusk with presents...

A cuckoo passes overhead – its distinct ka-ka-ka –
Please do not leave me alone.
I am utterly alone,
stuck on the last mountain of the world

And beyond me just one more mountain
where they say a deity lives
guarding a tiny turquoise lake.
And thereafter nothing but
realm of melting snows
where the souls of the gods live.

## Father

My hairs go aflame
as he hiccups and breathes the last of this earth.

A gray wart appears on my forehead.

I clasp your cold palms
to feel blackout of your blood vessels.

On your chest I burst
a silent pitcher of my life's sleep

Darkness,
a savage silence of *Sunya's* eternal ocean.

I glisten your rubbery body
from honey, curd and milk of seven rivers;

a tear keeps rolling endlessly
on the naked wound of my secret grief.

For the last time I hold
this face of yours in my trembling hands;

blast of a wail
ravages sunlight of my faith.

On your body I place
heavy logs damp from a history of vanquished hearts.

In the crack of your still mouth
I drop grain of a rainbow

and light the last fire
that shall blacken quiet pages of my youth.

I hit the center of your skull
aflame in the spluttering pyre

to ignite a bejeweled passage to eternity.

On the flooded banks of the Ganges
I knead your limbs all over again;

I make your head
heart, hands, life-veins, lines of your fate.

From the mantras of my breaths
I feed hunger of your blood vessels

and see you go alone
along the blazing fields of *Garuda Purana*

eating crumbs of the blessed food
lost in the memories of my childhood

when you lifted me
up in the fragrant stretch of the blue hillside air

and probably for the first time
in your life, smiled...

# "At Forty You Die"

At forty two moons start throbbing
like bright eyes of your own children.
At forty two people you dream of
most frequently, two people who dreamt
of you and your eyes all their lives.

At forty in the early
dawn of your desperate decades
you start dreaming of your mother first.

She comes limping
like a wounded cockroach
from the other world
to clasp your sweaty palms
to kiss your eyebrows
withering under the blind stare
of a merciless sun,
to complains of the tulips that faded
under the blind stare of a merciless sun.

At forty you dream
of your father frequently,
a Buddha or an exhausted god,
a lion repentant for a lifetime,
a familiar stranger who made you
what you are in your dreams
and left you alone,
bleeding on the mule-paths of life.
At forty you see him everywhere,
in the creases of your skin,
in the puffed-out eyelids,
in the fluffy temples
where two crescent moons appear,
silvery and savage like ensuing life's itinerary.

At forty he lusts in the crazed
fields of your blood vessels.
He escorts you to
the open spaces of his cherished riverbanks

pavilions of tantric priests
ashrams of ascetics before bonfires of annihilation.
He guides you to the bog lands
of his fond memories where once
his beloved woman lived and
then left him, one by one,
"Forgot the old chums, fell in the trap of new ones"

She comes limping
like a wounded cockroach
from the other world
to clasp your sweaty palms
to kiss your eyebrows
withering under the blind stare
of a merciless sun
to complain of the tulips that faded
under the blind stare of a merciless sun.

At forty your own woman's mouth
starts smelling of deceit,
a Bhairab's mask,
a masculine leer along
the canyons of her body.

At forty you start
questioning questions
and decide to die
like one dies in poetry or books.
Or proverbs that proved false—
*People above forty should be shot dead.*

You resolve what you didn't all life long—
to reach out to touch
the rim of unheard horizons
elusive Shangri-la from where no return
to exquisite valleys of life is possible.

But your children's eyes start
shining like burning stars
along the moons of your secret lusts.

At forty you die to be born again
and again in the theatre of your children's eyes.

## Eyes of Andreas' Chorten

Very human, hungry,
feeble, almost,

water like, fish like,
a just born baby's tear like

a charcoal geometry
on the palpable face of an upright glacier

pure and crystalline
Christ like, before Paul's murky shadow fell,

bemused eyes
older than horoscope of Siddhartha,

larger than the ocean
a female Yeti would have shed

before she was grabbed
and butchered by the monks

defeated by
the daggers of compassion

yantras of Sunya,
throttled by Boddhisattvas

brutally wounded,
weary eyes of a human

buried beneath
debris of spiritual flagstones

and snow sheets
of savage civilizations

a ruthless tear
in a body, a bullet full of blood,

a rough hewn
creature grabbed first

thing in the morning
like Ganesha's head

and crucified before
it could have said a word

about history of mystery,
hunger and humanity.

## The Letter

In harsh alpine valleys
I walked for days and weeks
meeting no one except
voices of my own ancestors
griffon-beaked visions from my secret lives
tattered souls fluttering
like threadbare prayer flags of peace,
unshaved, unwashed,
smelling like my grandpa in his last days
afraid of snow bites and meningitis
my heavy shoes dangling
like dead albatrosses around my neck,
bleary-eyed, worn-out
brooding over her sudden disappearance
from the cradle of my life's courtyard
groggy in company of angular angels
grizzly bear and golden eagles
touching the throbbing beats of
wounded mules, their flaccid faces crushed
like moldy beaten rice served
by almond eyed girls with bodies

bright enough to shame an Aphrodite,
offering me salt and rice and chilies
in their makeshift kitchens
along the salt route...

In harsh alpine valleys
after days and weeks of walking
I reached a village beneath shadow
of hushed glaciers where
a mother in threadbare cloak
her eyes, dimly lit lamps
in the flooded terraces of wrinkles
shyly pulled from her blue waistband
a crumpled piece of paper
splotched in Devanagri
glazed from sand grains of a seething desert

a dispatch reeking of blood, tears
and time bombs

a correspondence for me to read

a letter from her son
long lost to the battlefields of Afghanistan...

## Lost in the Annapurnas

*for Sukrity, Rachel and Alison*

Lost a T- shirt
near a crystal waterfall

a notebook
with names of birds and shamans of the canyons

finches, larks and red billed coughs
swifts, lammergeiers, griffins and redstarts

my rainbow colored umbrella
with flowers and million butterflies trapped in it

one of the lens
of my looking glass in a pond at Hot springs

lost excess fat,
double chin, pouch of my belly,

drooling flesh of my cheekbones
lost worries of my city struggles

in the leech-greasy forests,
oak and maple, conifers and rhododendrons

threw a copy of the bestseller
over the rusty bars of a squeaking wooden ridge

for the bearded goats
of the famed valleys to read and rejoice

lost fears
of finding right words
perfect dreams,
faultless partners along

narrow cliffside tracts
skirting utter horror of highest precipices

lost my unease
along with my troubled heart

to the glaciers
of Annapurnas...

# NINE

# Robin S Ngangom

A bilingual poet and translator, **Robin S Ngangom** was born in Imphal, Manipur, in 1959. He has published three books of poetry, *Words and the Silence*, *Time's Crossroads*, and *The Desire of Roots*. His poems and translations have appeared in literary journals and anthologies such as *The New Statesman*, *Verse*, *Planet: The Welsh Internationalist*, *The Literary Review*, *Kavya Bharati* , *Chandrabhaga* and *Indian Literature*. He has received numerous awards including the Udaya Bharati National Award for poetry.

## Primary Schools

I remember only the detritus of schools
which taught fear,
where only nuns seemed to believe
in the power of the written word and punishment.
There was a boy in the middle of it all
who once forged his father's signature
in order to dodge a maths test
and spent the whole day in a World War II cemetery
sleeping between roses and epitaphs.
The intimidation of books from Glasgow
made him steal small notes and coins from his father
which admitted him to a mystic circle
of titbits, cannabis, and adult tales
far away from pink rooms and uniform handwriting
or 'eena meena maina mo' by rote
after clambering walls that grow glass-creepers
to the freedom of cork trees and frogs and egrets,
a stinking marshy world of catapults and running noses
which grappled with black polished shoes
and moral science, to return home
on cloudy evenings brewing storm-fuelled nights
exiled on a reed mat and only a hurricane lamp
with slate, chalk, and as the years grew up
inkwell and bamboo-pulp paper
were the keepsakes of his childhood.
There were mosquito storms and
cool dirt floors polished with cow dung and clay,
ruined walls and lizard myrtles and moss
which reminded elders of neglect
near a big water tank left behind by British soldiers
where vipers came to drink, and
gaudy walls of goddesses.

I can see the naïve boy
who couldn't read the dirty word
spelt on the ground by his older friends

in the calligraphy of randy boyhood,
and, later, obsessed with that moist idea
explored his girl cousins fervently.

There were long delightful, convalescent afternoons
of illustrated classics without
the stress of the school bus when he heard
only the sleepy clang of hammers
in the nearby smithy, when life burnt slowly
like calories even when he was sleeping,
without the solemnity of anyone's life
coming to an end.

## To a Woman from Southeastern Hills

Woman with the soft voice
whispering wind among trees
I know why you run away from me,
fading from leaf to hill,
pursued by my tarnished name.
I who was born at an unearthly hour,
a sibling of light and darkness,
a freak among practical men,
a composer of bitter verse.
But you only tossed your riverine hair
and earth moves again on its wistful axis,
while a river flows hushed in an underground heart.

You, woman, from southeastern hills,
cloud-covered mystery, gliding on rain,
deep drink of rice wine with eyes closed,
child of the dancing bamboo, unction
of ginger on the wagging tongue.
Your voice is soft because mountain streams
taught your heart.

Tonight, a full moon steals above northern pines,

and boys from your native land sit on terraces
with their dolorous guitars, singing of loves
lost in the ravines of the heart.
I am that plaintive cry you did not wish to hear,
the love song you've exiled.
Even now my dreams sprout wings
among our impassive people, circling
in the wind with sad pride and faraway months,
ready to die and be trampled in mud.
In you, woman, from southeastern hills
all our memories gather into trembling hopes,
taking us back to a time before they gave us
religion to divide us, before the politician-priests
who laboured for their own redemption,
mouthing the name of god among benighted heathens.

Time before science, civilized laws and rock music,
time in the memory of gods.
Before coat and before nylon, bare-bosomed time,
time of the *puan* and story-telling cloak,
the running motif caught by fabric,
eloquent bead encircling your slender neck.
You, woman, on your father's terrace, a loom
hugging your hips, singing with the dancing
shuttle in your hand, you offered me tobacco.
In afternoons you return with water humming
in the bamboo and asked if I were thirsty.
That was the time of the weretiger, before
temples and churches, time of the freethinking
dormitory, when boys trained in the school of
the warrior, time of the daring headhunter,
when legends could not wait to be born, and
places were named. And time before this
English tongue we speak now.

Forgetfulness of being afflict us.
Let us refuse these names, woman,
our names we proudly put down on pages,
these names that come between our lips

cold as parchment. They can never learn
our songs, or feel the drumbeats of our hearts.
How would they harness the rivers
in our blood, rushing without boundaries,
or tame our precipices and sullen fields?

Will you, woman, devastate these dreams
as men ravage the hills, leaving only
scars and litter behind, after all hopes
have been mined? Woman, from the land
of *Chhura,* our roots suck from the
same liquid tongue. Because of these
shared dreams and waters, none knows you
like I do. I who can nurture the twin syllables
of your name. Speak again, woman,
with your dulcet tongue, for this is the desire
of these hills and yearning stones.

—

*Puan*: a traditional sarong-style dress worn by Mizo women.
*Chhura* is the name of a popular Mizo folk-hero.

## Revolutionaries

### I

Before they used terror when things were beginning to go out of control and people showed aberrant behaviour, revolutionaries had asked poets in their lower ranks to compose patriotic songs for a country which cannot be found on any map. They would coerce nocturnal drivers of interstate buses to play tapes of one-act plays which are designed to make unsuspecting passengers weep with patriotic shame. I know this for real, I grew up with revolutionaries. They had even asked me to translate a press release over the phone.

Before he became the sharpshooter of a revolutionary band my childhood friend smelled of straw and cattle, and then one day he bridled a horse and rode it hard through a busy marketplace scattering customers and traders alike like straw in a gale. I was told that he buried a pistol at my cousin's backyard just before he went under the ground. Only after he came over ground with the venerable title 'teacher', because Chinese masters trained him, did I meet him on the street and he smelled of designer clothes. He now keeps himself occupied with work contracted out by the public works department and once asked me if I were married. He has two wives, one of them an actor.

Before the crackling fire of revolution which warms the hearts of boys we sat in a circle and talked endlessly about oppressors and life in the jungle. Friends brought stories of the ordained, who survived on roots and eggshells. We looked at Che's hammock with longing and even mixed his cocktail but had no idea of when to dig a tank pit. When little books with a star and red skins appeared it was too late for me. I had fallen in love, and although it broke my heart, my father sent me to another land with gentle hills, so that I can read other books which will make me stand on my bourgeois feet.

**II**

When they are not around they become butts of fun. The roving story then was of a wastrel who went home after midnight because he had wasted all his time with his layabout friends around a fire one winter night. He had to cross a walled house guarded by fierce dogs to reach his home. When the owner of the house who was woken up by the dogs asked "Who goes there?" the wastrel found his wits and replied, "In the service of the motherland" in a solemn voice as one would expect a revolutionary to reply.

When they became arbiters when someone's duck was stolen or two women were fighting over one man I stopped being furious with them.

You should write when you can still laugh at yourself and the world, before you give yourself up to despair.

# Gangtok, February 1998

*for Guru T Ladakhi*

Call of faraway snow in the eye of a wish.
When we contemplate your emerald tongue
quivering on pale sand and rock
we grow more weary of striving cities
and desultory roads. But you will
teach us to name the forest and the mountain,
indignant one, who will not wait.
Teesta, tell me the meaning of your name.
Like secretive men impelled by a sinuous love
we follow your scent when the flame of the forest
borrows a monk's robes and something shimmers
beneath the veil of the Himalayan sky
until you lift us on your fraternal lap
of flowers and stone, Gangtok.

## II

Who are the artisans of wood that left
no names on the palace gate of the Chogyal?
A misty forest looks up the face of a sheer drop
where the king's men punished hardened criminals
tied up in sacks, by pushing them off this cliff,
so the stories insinuate. The royalty since then
has paid its price to a nation which humbled them
through treachery, so history moralizes. And this
is where a landslide took many by surprise.
A lanky building just slipped off
and lay on its face like a drunk,
and only the prayer flags
stand here to appease the difficult gods.
I look where the mountains keep their enigmatic silence
and climb stairs which lead to the doors of the sky,
and rain entered the afternoon without invitation.

## III

5am one whisky-coated morning
and Khangchendzonga appeared, bust translucent
like a forgotten model, her face quickly
obscured by a cirrus of snow,
provoked by a jealous sunstone
cast on her proud forehead.

In the aquamarine afternoon
Rumtek turns slow prayer wheels
which cuts across the axis of earth
to generate compassion for a cold-blooded world.
The Karmapa who fled Tibet
reconstructed this arabesque seat of learning
from adoration and spotless memory.
We remove shoes and enter a hooded door
to find butter statues meditating
in all the shades of earth.
Thus flesh will melt one day
to yield the running colours of earth.
An intonation of monks
and the deep drone of drums
heighten the mystery of reincarnation each moment.
But what does one seek from the illuminate
if the wayward mind must be conquered first?
A grimy gap-toothed Tibetan comes begging
while young acolytes scurry to fetch water,
as the world of appearance marked time.
Adornment, renunciation, ego, alms,
where is there a life without desire?

## IV

5pm when evenings crumble from Himalayan snow
Gangtok folds us in her breast.
We leave melancholy outside Zam-den,
where positive elements converge,
and song and dance and poetry
find a home.

## When You Do Not Return

When you leave your native hills
winter is merely a reminder
of all past winters, of all
the loves we lost, and there's none
to care for the old and infirm. All
the hospices have closed their doors.

Leaves no longer respond
to the alchemy of seasons,
and the heart lies fallow
expecting winter rain. Earth
has closed again like a woman
when you do not return, and dreams
turn to rust, the flame and the dew
cannot create art. Only lust breaks
on the branches of night, and men
wear hideous masks, the fragrance
of the wild rose is lost, and only
the flowers of the market are on sale.

The poet loses his metaphors
when you do not return, and he
merely repeats himself in the
dreadful arithmetic of the day.
The world knew me as happy when
you gave me your healing hand
and now ignores my grief because
you left. The murmuring river
is hushed as it loses its course
in a sunless kingdom.

When you leave your native land
messianic young men betray principles,
and there's no fire in their eyes.
In the streets students shout themselves
hoarse for newly-arrived patriots. The

right and the left have become synonymous,
and citizens garland only the thieves.
The man of god merely chants the
sanctimonious burlesque of prayers,
while the poor remain cold and naked
the preacher is warm and fed. When
you do not return dead waters breed
reptiles in our minds, gunfire reverberates
in the hills, and bullets sprout from
windows instead of geraniums. When you
do not return after the bloodthirsty purges,
flies swarm around limp flags. The barbwire
of the day encloses us as we enter the era
of the assassin.

When you leave your native hills
I can only speak of lost times,
and of sorrow and blood. And I write
these letters of winter, asking you
to return again to the hills, on
grey pages I send you happiness
because it has left my home.

## Last Word

What kind of a poet is he, they ask.
I said: 'I am a poet of earth and space,
possibly water, but not fire. I know
my limitations, and there are many things
between earth and sky I cannot name.
I have an ancient desire for understanding,
meaninglessness frightens me.
That is why I love simple things
such as sunlight on our shoulders,
or women with firm breasts
and hills quiet in the rain.'
They whispered among themselves:

'How come his poetry is riddled with bullets then?'
So I said:
'I wanted my poems to exude a heady odour
but only the sweet taint of blood
or burning flesh emanates from my poem.'
Then they said:
'His poems are always falling from arrogant heights.'
I answered:
'I've always wanted to see them fall
like leaves which turn beautiful before they die.'
But they said:
'When they fall his poems would shatter
because he drops them on stony ground.'
I only said:
'I wanted them to fall like pebbles
into a pool. I'm sorry I always break
my words on hostile surfaces.'
Finally they said:
'That is why his poetry is guarded.
He courts death and freedom but his words
need protection by an armed escort.
He could not speak and allowed
muteness to bind his heart.
This is the origin of his fear.'

## After 'Jashn-e-Azadi'

(a film on Kashmir by Sanjay Kak)

The kite transforming into smoke lacing
The *chinars* is not a symbol.
The rose has migrated from the garden of paradise.
Freedom will never come
Poured into goblets waiting to be raised,
Martyrdom is a handout from god the hagiographer.
Only poetry of ruins is real.
The incoherent rose still blooms
From some beloved breast torn open.

## Flight

The warning disguised as a message
came before the village was up and about,
and when they left
they didn't carry pots or blankets
or even machetes.
As they went to the outpost of guardians
they left chickens running in the yard
and the dog lazing on the steps.

Flights like theirs
Do not have destinations,
And only once did they wish for wings.

The taste of the herd will return them
To dark and dingy towns where
They will sell used clothes, wild meat and herbs.
The most vulnerable will sell bodies.
Because in spite of the land mines
They still shared limbs.

Words like "the end of history"
Will not resonate anywhere in their lives.
They do not have meat and drinks left
To offer to embedded scribes
And newspapers have died on them. As before
Their fates will go unreported, arousing
Only a shred of curiosity somewhere.

## Body

Because I couldn't examine it from close quarters
Like Burton with his magnifying glass
I worshipped it from afar.
The body is never free of the human condition

And either weeps or sings, or becomes restive
If denied bacchanalia or tragedy.
Time is not its enemy as Ovid would have it
But the mind with its dark pledges.
If you kick it as Descartes demonstrated
It reacts violently, for it isn't the soul which replies
But flesh and bone with their
Entire moral and philosophical apparatuses.
The body is the key to Adam's children,
Heathen matter that mystics want to defeat.
Serial killers want to destroy it
As it often turns up in court as witness,
Rapists in uniform want to reduce it to pulp
Because it conceals intimate evidence,
Poets want to disembody it to elegize fallen man.
But the body is the sum of its parts,
Sever an organ but the tongue takes over,
Remove a hand and the foot starts painting,
Deny eyes and fingers are already on the keys.

## Guitar

Blue notes rising from its inviting hip
Of mahogany and rosewood
She voyaged from languid Rome
Like a cithara
On a slave ship to the South
Picking the rhythm of cotton
Heeding the call and response
Of deep African forests
Electrifying freight trains of night
On the calloused fingers
Of a hobo fleeing the plantation
With only the neck of a bottle
To give crying and dancing
New eloquence.

He also chased a flaming red skirt
All the way from Andalusia
To Cuba
Only to be carried off by the leader
Of a band of terrorists soothing
His killer-comrades under moonlit pines
In Northeast India with heartstrings of steel.

## Laitlum

I treasure you for the jealousy you've hatched,
the afterglow that deceived me in your noontide arms.
I want you with the pain of a green luminosity
or the warm shock of the myrrh of pines,
choking back ambuscade passions
I want to be converted amongst houses kneeling
in the thick of firs of former times,
carelessly strewn without electricity.

Shrouded wine of the ravine's murmuring epilogue,
swaying with your body's innocent betrayal,
before a spellbound audience of rustic animals
we're travelling invisibly from age towards youth.

When you sealed your fate to mine
I discovered roads we had misplaced,
dark wet in the twilight's excited face,
wayside stalls opening iridescent eyes,
watery fields newly laid in olive yearning and see
wisps of happiness wafting down the pines.

TEN

# Kynpham Sing Nongkynrih

**Kynpham Sing Nongkynrih** was born in Sohra (Cherrapunjee), Meghalaya, in 1964. He has published three poetry collections in Khasi and two poetry collections in English. Recipient of several national awards, he is an Associate Professor at the Department of English, North-Eastern Hill University, Shillong, where he lives.

## Blasphemous Lines for Mother

R. K. Narayan is dead.
Tonight he sits pensive
in his bamboo chair
talking of a "very rare soul".

Suddenly seized by a desire
to vivisect his own "very rare soul"
from end to end, he proclaims:

My mother is more "plain-dealing",
more "truth-telling" than Narayan's.
My mother is retired, toothless, diabetic,
and bedevilled by headaches and a blinding cataract.
In short, she is a cantankerous old woman.

I remember the time when she was a cantankerous
young woman. When she took an afternoon nap,
she was tigerish: "You sons of a vagina!" she
would snarl, "you won't even let me rest for a
moment, sons of a fiend! Come here sons of a beast!
If I get you I'll lame you! I'll maim you! ... Sons
of a louse! You feed on the flesh that breeds you!
Make a sound again when I sleep and I'll thrash you
till you howl like a dog! You irresponsible nitwits!
how will I play the numbers if I don't get a good
dream?[1] How will I feed you, sons of a lowbred?"

And this fiery salvo would come hurtling
with wooden stools, iron tongs and bronze
blowers, as we ran for our lives and she
gave chase with canes and firewood,
her hair flying loose, her eyes inflamed
and her tongue lashing with a mad rage.
And we being but children would never
learn anything except becoming experts
at dodging her unconventional weapons.

I remember how, having no daughter, she would
make me wash her blood-stained rags. Refusal
was out of the question. So, always I would pick
them with sticks and pestle them in an old iron
bucket till the water cleared. But mind you, all this on
the sly. Seeing me not using my hands would be lethal.

Those days in Cherra we never knew what
a toilet was. We never had a septic tank
or a service latrine. We simply did our job
in our sacred groves.[2] But sometimes
my mother would do her job in a trash can.
Then it would fall on me to ferry the cargo
to a sacred grove. Refusal was out
of the question. So, always I would sprinkle
ash upon it, top it with betel-nut peels
and things and do my best to avoid nosy
neighbours and playmates. Those who
have seen Kamal Hasan in *Pushpak*
will understand my stratagems.

I could cite a thousand and one things
to demonstrate how cantankerously
rare my mother is. And I decline
to tell you anything good about her.
I'm not a Narayan and I decline
to tell you how she suffered when
my bibulous father was alive; or how
she suffered when he died; or how
she suffered rearing her two sons
and her dead sister's toddlers
in the proper way. There's only one
thing commendable I will admit about her:
if she had married again and not been
the cantankerous woman that she is,
I probably would not be standing
here reading this poem today.

[1]Archery gambling. Some people would buy a number based on the interpretation of their dreams. [2] Community forests, prohibited through sanctification, found in almost every village in the Khasi Hills of Meghalaya. [3] A popular South Indian silent movie starring Kamal Hasan as a kidnapper, who tries every morning to get rid of his prisoner's excrement in ingenious ways.

# Funeral Speech

*"De mortuis nil nisi bonum".* –Latin proverb

Funerals are places where I stand aloof
amidst whispers, hush-toned gossips, and
stifled chuckles; bowing my head, looking
at my shoes, or turning heavenwards with
vacant eyes, listening to vigorous homilies
and songs, drowning all wailings.

But once, the usual did not happen: once
I was asked to deliver a funeral speech.

I began to daydream.

Friends, neighbours, kith and kin,
*Bah* [1] Robin was a good office-goer
and very much a gentleman.
Soft-spoken and mild-mannered,
he never had a harsh word for anyone.
But very sad to say, he listened
to the tavern's song and began walking
like a seismograph. His eyes took on
the rustiness of *kwai* [2] stain, the watery glaze
of a nitwit. His head became the tangled
nest of a crow, his cheeks a pair of buttocks
and his nose a tomato that dripped so
consistently that the teeth of an elephant
seemed to grow from his nostrils. His
lips were moist and bloated like rotten
brinjals, his teeth like a dog's feasting
on excrement, his breath like menstrual blood
and his body smell like the scent of a cobra.

In this way he led a most despicable
and miserable life, speaking the language
of A-category auditors and deserting his
wife and only daughter. For the last fifteen

years he had so devotedly given himself up
to drink that his medical report said
there was no more blood in his alcohol.

What good could be said about him now?
Friends used to say he had a neat
handwriting, but what...

Jolted out of my reverie and reminded
of my duty, I recoiled in horror
and left in a hurry.

*[1]Mister. [2] Blood red stain of betel nut normally taken together with betel leaf, lime and tobacco.*

## Self-actualisation

Like Shelley with his "blithe spirit"
I have often tried to understand
this man who is named Kynpham.

How should I describe myself?

A son of a crab, since I fail to suffer
my mother's temper, who, living in my
house, treats me as one of her tenants.

An abusive husband, since I decline to be
tamed in a matrilineal arrangement.
A devoted husband, since beautiful women
are intimidating and no one knows
I seek even now, the woman, who if found,
would be the ruin of my life.

A wicked neighbour, since I object to a toilet
being built against my compound wall and bark
at window-breaking locality boys.

A felonious councillor, since I attend the village
*dorbar* [1] without a moustache. A guilty bystander,
since I make myself small as a mouse, even when
riffraff and drunks are drowning out all reason.

A bad relation, since I dislike
clan meetings and spurn playing
mother against aunt
brother against brother.

An 'evil' administrator, since I forbid
the staff to come at noon
and depart just after noon.

A Vice-Chancellor's *chamcha,* [2] since I chance
to be a Public Relations Officer and the academia
cannot tell between personal and official.

A recalcitrant Indian, since I am buried
too deep in my tribal roots and refuse to be
swept away by the Main Stream. A mutinous
Indian, since I protest to army occupation,
uranium mining, influx and *saffronisation.* [3]

A counterfeit scholar, since I write
only poetry, working in a university.

A small-time poet, since I cannot class myself
a small-town writer, since this town judges books
by the weight, and writers by their age.

A retrograde, since I want trees on the hills,
birds in the woods, fishes in the streams.
A heathen, since I believe in sacred groves.

An atheist, since I am not a Christian.
A heretic, since I believe in the humanity
of my conscience.

An enemy of the human race, since I believe
in animal rights and birth control. An advancer
of the Malthusian theory, since I wish to include
weapons of mass destruction in the list
of natural calamities.

A hopeless believer, since I know not what
is to be done with all that I believe. A hypocrite,
since I pursue private dreams and like a dog,
nod with the head and shake with the tail
to everything.

I shall describe myself as that supreme diplomat:
"I am who I am" and that is the ultimate enigma.

*[1]Khasi village council. Traditionally, drunks and men without a moustache are not allowed to participate. [2] a yes-man. [3] An attempt to apply fundamentalist Hindu principles to important national policies.*

## Hiraeth [1]

In the solemn hour of early morning the shrill chorus
of a *namaz* wrenched me from my affable dreams.
I twisted and turned and finally gave up.

No more do I hear the morning sounds of home:
birds warbling, cicadas whining, crows cawing,
chickens yapping about the yard and my uncle
readying for the cement factory. Twisting and turning
I understood the *hiraeth* of Soso, [2] who wished
no more than to be a boy once more. I miss that too,
and our old rooster, how his triumphant cry would stir
my slumber making me draw closer to mother.

Out of that restlessness the past rises from dimly
remembered songs and I watch my ghostly ancestors
hasten from their dark pallets at the rooster's
first reveille; warming up for their fields,

boiling rice, packing their midday meal in leaves.
I saw them arm themselves with hook-like whetted
knives at the second. And slinging bamboo cones
on bamboo straps, I watch them emerge from their huts
at the third; bamboo torches twinkling in their hands,
ancient songs and playful limericks flowing
from their lips.

Now, in the cycle of a year
my sleep is often startled
by raucous *azaans*, jangling bells,
wild ululations, weird conch-shells
midnight carousals, spirituous carols,
clamorous crackers, nocturnal heavy metals.

Strange sounds are crowding this town.
Like the rooster, I too, seem
to have become obsolete.

[1] Welsh word, loosely translated as various forms of longing.
[2] Soso Tham, chief bard of the Khasis.

## When the Prime Minister Visits Shillong the Bamboos Watch in Silence

When the Prime Minister
planned a visit to the city
bamboo poles sprang up from pavements
like a welcoming committee.

But when he came, he was
only the strident sounds of sirens
like warnings in war-time bombings.

The bamboos watched in silence.

He came with twin objectives
a mission for peace and progress.

But he was a rumbling in the clouds
a prattle in the air.

And some say he came
homing in like a missile
and left flying like an arrow.

In-between?

Some say he dropped
like a falling star
and was sighted by a few
disgruntled leaders.

He came like a threat
and scam-stained ministers
were in a cold sweat.
But he left like a defused bomb.

They wondered
what he could have seen
of the land
what of the people
he could have learnt
when he came
like the snapping of fingers.

They wondered
and sought answers
like little children.

Only the bamboos watched in silence
too used to the antics of men.

## Rain Song 2000

*(To the Poets Who Have Left)*

The April sky has taken us all by surprise
spouting incessantly for the last many days.

I scanned the papers.
No depression in the Bay of Bengal.
No cyclone in Bangladesh.
Only violence in Bihar bye-elections
and ISI agents in the Northeast region.
Down the page are politicians grinning
like potholes, spinning their ancient web
to an ancient bunch of sycophants.
There is a woman lynching
her children and executing suicide.
There are teachers threatening strikes
protests against price hikes
outcries over custodial deaths.
A *nokma*[1] is gunned down
an SP is shot at
a tradesman is kidnapped
some militants have been nabbed.

But these are no more than fillers:
so why is the sky weeping
a river of unseasonable tears?
Why is the wind shrieking night and day
and pines beating their chests in pain?

I asked a learned man.
He quoted scientific reasons
spitfiring them one by one.
Global warming, charcoal burning
the ozone layer, polythene bags
ecological imbalances, Jaiñtia coal mines
timber trade, *jhum* [2] cultivation
West Khasi uranium and on and on.

But religious men were convinced
the world is too riddled with sin.
Hindus have gored too many good Samaritans.
Christians have forced too many conversions
and cocksure Seng Khasi [3] should not
have ascended our holy mountain, Sohpet Bneng.

As I lay on my bed
processing this input
the darkness blazed, the sky
was bombarded with thunder
and it wept once again
as the wind gave it
a million lashes.

The churlish wind broke in
through the skylight
and booed with disdain.
But I listened to the rain
sizzling on the roof
and suddenly I heard
my heart sighing:

the hills are spurning too many
of those who love them
for a baneful breed of migratory men.

[1] Garo headman. [2] Traditional slash and burn technique of cultivation.
[3] Organisation considered as custodian of the Khasi heritage and indigenous faith. The cockerel is its revered symbol.

## Laitkynsew [1]

This New Year's midnight, 2005,
people no longer craned their necks
like roosters at the sound of crackers.

Troubles are no longer social,
at least not now that our jungle rovers

are merely roving the city streets,
armless without arms.

From Mumbai, Arvik sent me peace and poetry.
Certainly, brutal hegemony must end.
Certainly, missiles and car bombs must be silent.
I'm neither with the one nor the other.
But sad, Arvik! wishing for peace is like wishing
for heaven, and I have stopped dreaming
since the woman who opened my heart like a pear tree
in early spring also became the winter of its barrenness.
Wish as you might, I doubt if poetry could ever flourish
in peace, or that I could ever turn from lament to praise.

Troubles are no longer social,
at least not for us since calamities
are experienced only as live telecasts.

As the sea spits humans like bad food,
we burst in revelry, watching stars
explode in our faces.

I have come to this village perched above
the deep distant gorges of my hometown
to escape the bludgeoning mawkishness of tragedy.

Very grudgingly, I had allowed the deduction
of a day's salary. But to all those who came for more,
I merely said, "Nature must shake off its burden
or crumble and die like an overworked beast."
And then, "How would I know that what we give
is what they will get?"

But now I have come here, for in the face of this carnage,
my convictions would only have turned me into a scoundrel.

The Archbishop of Canterbury had launched a searing sermon:
"The question, 'How can you believe in a God who permits
suffering on this scale?' is, therefore, very much around

at the moment, and it would be surprising if it weren't—
indeed it would be wrong if it weren't".
The Pope had produced a predictable answer:
"Faith teaches us that even during the most difficult
and painful of tests… God will never abandon us".

I'm getting away from these too,
from questions and justifications,
and of course, from the sickening head count,
as if this thing from the ocean
is just another Master Blaster,
already making two centuries and a half
and fast heading for the triple tons. [2]

I have come here to rinse and replenish my thoughts,
to forget all the little irritants of my days, only to find
too much forgetfulness. The bells ring with the glory
of an alien land, and as we swallow the holiness
of unknown deserts and follow the history of the Diaspora,
nobody can tell me the meaning of your name.

Laitkynsew! today I will plumb the depths
of your tangled ravines. He who has not trodden
the rock bottom of these precipices can never claim
he really knows his land.

The sweet smell of burnt grass; the crackle of burnt tinder;
the cerulean smoke raising its flag of cinder; the orange flames
feasting raucously, all together, all at once like bratlings;
the motley grasshoppers scattering, fleeing their homes
like those poor Palestinians— I'm beginning to remember
my childhood again. This, my children, is what we call *"saiñding"*
fighting fire with fire.

The jungle is a village enclosing villages, crisscrossed
by ancient pathways, fed by shadowy springs running
through split bamboos like flyovers in cities. In this village,
the silence is its peace; the soft rivulets, its secrets;

the songbirds, its celebration; the boulder-strewn rivers,
its magnificence. In this village, the living roots of rubber trees
are the lifeblood.

*Ficus elastica*! "Living-root Bridges", "Living-root Ladder Bridges",
and Nongriat, "The Double-decker Root Bridge"! Feast your eyes,
behold the magnificent gift of the jungle, the simple genius
of the old ones, the hand of man guiding the artistry of Mother Earth,
shaping this crown and breathing beauty of the ancient world.
The Japanese hail this entwining treasure, "A bio-engineering wonder,
the only kind in the world". [3] Gaze upon it, the land's "enlightenment" [4]
we must seek; the glory we must acknowledge; the hymn we must sing.
This is the legacy we must leave: not bombs and impossible causes;
nor flashy cars and concrete structures, the targets of all our ambitions,
the decay of our lives. I would like to grow upwards like this shaggy spirit
of the gorges, branching outwards, laying a bridge that is the living root
of the race, the link between times and generations, the lifeline
of ages gone, the reminder of how well we had lived and had served.

I have learnt so much from this jungle, simple things
like the name of "*Phandieng*", tree-potato, with its tall thin stem
and its stout tuberous root. I have learnt to differentiate
between green and wild pepper. I have seen the flaming áreca-nut
dangling in bunches from the tousle top of its branchless tree,
straight and smooth as a lamp post. I have followed the path
of the betel-leaf as it creeps along the forest floor and up
the moss-enfolded trunks for a peep at the sky. I have seen birds
that I have only heard of. I have listened to the soft cajoling
of *Ki Slang*, the melodies of *Jlaeit*, the distressed call of *Jyllob*,
the ominous rumble of *Pohkrong* and the forlorn sadness of *Kairiang*.[5]

I have watched girls of bewitching loveliness
flitting from tree to tree, giving us a shy smile
from their wood-shaded huts. How I wish
I could pluck these "half-hidden" violets
to keep them in my flower pots!

I have come to understand the incredible bountifulness

of this place, and its incredible hardship
as my limbs tremble from mere descending and ascending.

In the late afternoon bees swarm about their crevice hives,
buzzing in from the four winds, delivering their cargo of nectar.
As they hover like helicopters amidst the confused drone
of their wings, it seems to me that these divine manufacturers,
like the entire planet, are also air-dropping Tsunami-relief materials.
Yes, I too shall go gather some bee-water.

Villages stuck into the cliff face like glow-worms,
floating in the dark void like a reflection of stars
and cruise ships in the sea.
I have come here feeling like a kitchen rag,
only to emerge from the jungle with the taste of ripe fruits
and the scent of bay leaf forever in my soul.

[1] The name of a village near Sohra. It overlooks the many wooded canyons running down towards Bangladesh. [2] According to theage.com.au, as of 10 February 2005, the Tsunami death toll was placed at around 296,000. [3] See www.cherraresort.com. [4]A message from Soso Tham's major poem. Tham was the chief bard of the Khasis. [5] *Ki Slang, Jlaeit, Jyllob, Pohkrong* and *Kairiang* are names of popular songbirds.

## Pain

*"Even as the stone of the fruit must break, that its heart may stand in the sun, so must you know pain".*
– Kahlil Gibran

Alone on a birthday
I went out to the quiet evening
to watch the early moon.

Upon the hills
the jacarandas wore blue

and willows stood with bowed heads
before the stumps of native pines.

There are many things
to be sad about in this life
many things that become a misfortune
many things I would like to thresh
like a washerman
with the aroma of sweet soaps
on the smooth washing stones.

There was not much pain at my birth
not much pain at any single event.

Pain grows with years
deepens like a blemish
and wraps around life
like this cruel mismatch.

Upon the hills
the fireflies twinkled
and the early moon waited
creeping silently across the sky.

In the gathering gloom
I watched the early moon, waiting
for the night to thicken.

# Nirala Series

*A Series of Contemporary Writing*

**TEN: The New Indian Poets**
*Selected and Edited by*
**Jayanta Mahapatra & Yuyutsu Sharma**
ISBN-81-8250-025-7 2013 pp.134 Hard

**Milarepa's Bones, Helambu**
33 New Poems
**Yuyutsu RD Sharma**
ISBN-81-8250-032-X 2012 Hard pp.82

**Garuda** & Other Poems of Astral Plains
**David B. Austell**
ISBN-81-8250-038-9 2012 Hard pp.64

**Inside Out, Upside Down, & Round and Round**
Poems Selected & New
**John J. Trause**
ISBN-81-8250-049-4 2012 Paper pp.83

**All the way from Kathmandu**
Selected Jazz Poems
**John Clarke**
ISBN-81-8250-042-7 2012 Paper pp.82

**No Child More Perfect** & Other Poems
**Christi Shannon Kline**
ISBN-81-8250-039-7 2012 Paper pp.82

# Acknowledgement

The anthology includes many new poems as well as some previously published. The poems, if previously, are reprinted from the following journals or books; all those reprinted from books are by permission of the publishers listed. Thanks are due to all the copyright holders cited below for their kind permission:

**Anupama Raju:** 'Born, again' from *Mosaic* (Unisun Publications, 2008), 'Tale of a Forest', 'No Borders', 'House of Dreams', from *Poetry With Prakriti,* (Prakriti Foundation, 2007-2008, 3), 'Tale of a Forest' and 'No Borders', first appeared in *Indian Literature,* ( Sahitya Akademi, May/June 2009) 'House of Dreams' first appeared in *The Little Magazine,* (Vol iv, Issue 4, 2003), 'No Borders', 'No1', 'Bombay Flats', 'Tale of a Forest', *Nine* (Daastaan). **Malovika Pawar :** 'At a Resthouse near Jhansi' and 'In a year of Burning ,1975' first appeared in *Virginia Quarterly Review,* 'Expatriate Love' and 'The Wolves are Circling the City' first appeared in *Chandrabhaga.* **Rumjhum Biswas:**'Small Town Road One Night' was first published in *Words-Myth* (UK, 2008), 'Desecration' first published in Pratilipi (India) July 2009 Issue, 'Monday Aubade' first published in *Poems Niederngasse* (Switzerland, 2007), 'Morning Encounter' was first published in *Indigo Dreams Anthology* (UK, 2010), Rapture of the Deep' first published in *A Little Poetry* (USA, 2007 – 08), 'Road Map' first published in *Southern Ocean* Review (New Zealand, 2006), 'The Other Side of the Sun' first published in *Mascara Literary Review* (Australia, 2009). **Nabanita Kanungo**: 'I was Born,' 'Mylliem Now' and 'Native Man,' first published in *Indian Literature,* (Sahitya Akademi,

Jul/Aug, 2009), "The Missing Tooth" first appeared in *Thoughts and Pen*, 'A Bend in Time' first published in *Museindia*, 2010, 32. **Rabindra K Swain:** 'Susurrus in the Skull', 'He has in Him', 'Over a Cup of Tea', 'Moths' and 'The Plight of Gods' from Susurrus in the Skull from (Authorspress, New Delhi,2008) first appeared in *The Kenyon Review*, The Times Literary Supplement, Kunapipi, Indian Literature, Acumen; 'Wall of Resistance' and 'Sons and Fathers' from Severed Cord (Indialog Publications, New Delhi, 2002) first appeared in Shenandoah, 'Anything Human is Proper' from *A Tapestry of Steps* (Orient Longman, Hyderabad, 1999) first appeared in *Lipi*; 'Stalks of Lotus' from *Once Back Home* (Har-Anand Publications, New Delhi, 1996) first appeared in *Critical Quarterly*; 'What You Miss' unpublished. **Sudeep Sen** : 'Mediteranean' first appeared in *New Writing 15* (Granta). 'Offering' first appeared in *Monsoon*, 'Bharatnatyam Dancer' first appeared in *Gentleman*, 'A Blank Letter' first appeared in *Language for a New Century* (Norton). 'Flying Home' first appeared in *Postmarked India: New & Selected Poems* (HarperCollins), 'Banyan' first appeared in *Initiate: Oxford New Writing* (Blackwell), 'Desire' first appeared in *Indian Love Poems* (Knopf/Random House/Everyman), 'Choice' first appeared in *The Literary Review and* 'Kargil' first appeared in *Platform*.**Yuyutsu Sharma:** 'Sherpa Mother' first appeared in *Everest Failures*, (Nirala, New Delhi), Mules', first appeared in *The Little Magazine*, New Delhi, 'At Forty You Die...' from *Space Cake Amsterdam and Other Poems of Europe and America*, (Howling Dog Press, Colorado), 'Father' from *Annapurna Poems:New and Selected*, (Nirala Publications, New Delhi), 'Little Paradise Lodge' first appeared in *Indian Literature*, Sahitya Academy, New Delhi, 'Eyes of Andreas' Chorten' first appeared in *www.WayToEverest.de: A photographic and Poetic Journey to the Foot of Everest*, (Epsilonmedia, Germany, 2006). 'Lost in Annapurnas' first appeared in *Modern Poetry in Translation*, (MPT, UK, 2012), 'The Letter' from *Milarepa's Bones, Helambu, 33 New Poems*, (Nirala, 2012). **Kynpham Sing Nongkynrih**: 'Laitkynsew' first published in PEN International, London, 2009; 'When the Prime Minister...' and 'Hiraeth' first published in *Poetry International Web*, Rotterdam, 2006.